W9-BIQ-878

621.8
TOC

Tocci, Salvatore.

Experiments with
friction.

$23.50                    34880030001585

| DATE | | |
|---|---|---|
| | | |
| | | |
| | | |
| | | |
| | | |
| | | |
| | | |
| | | |
| | | |
| | | |
| | | |
| | | |
| | | |

*Reading Consultant*
**Nanci R. Vargus, Ed.D**
*Primary Multiage Teacher*
*Decatur Township Schools*
*Indianapolis, Indiana*

*Science Consultant*
**Robert Gardner**

*The photo on the cover shows a speed skater. The photo on the title page shows American swimmer Nelson Diebel. Many swimmers shave their heads so they can cut down on resistance in the water and swim faster.*

**The author and publisher are not responsible for injuries or accidents that occur during or from any experiments. Experiments should be conducted in the presence of or with the help of an adult. Any instructions of the experiments that require the use of sharp, hot, or other unsafe items should be conducted by or with the help of an adult.**

Library of Congress Cataloging-in-Publication Data

Tocci, Salvatore.
Experiments with friction / Salvatore Tocci.
   p. cm. - - (A True Book)
   Includes biographical references and index.
   Summary: Explores the force of friction through ten simple experiments using everyday objects.
   ISBN 0-516-22512-X (lib. bdg.)    0-516-29363-X (pbk)
   1. Friction—Experiments—Juvenile literature. [1.Friction—Experiments. 2. Experiments.]  I. Title. II. Series.
QC197 .T63 2002
621.8'9'078—dc21
                                          2001004916

# Contents

# How Fast Can You Go?

When was the last time you went down a slide in a playground? Did you notice that you went slower and slower as you coasted down the slide? Did you also notice that the slide is much steeper near the top than it is near the bottom? This helps you slow down as you get closer to the bottom so that you don't go crashing into the ground.

Have you ever gone down a slide in a water park? If you have, then you probably noticed that you go down faster on a water slide than you do on a playground slide. On a playground slide, you almost stop by the time you get to the bottom. But on a water slide, you keep moving along quickly, even at the bottom.

Both water slides and playground slides have smooth

You can slide much faster down the water slide because water reduces friction.

surfaces. Both slides are sloped so that you go down them without stopping. So then why do you go down faster on a water slide? The water allows you to slide down faster because it reduces **friction**.

# What Is Friction?

Have you ever stood on a steep hill? It may have been so slanted that you felt as if you were going to start sliding down it. But you kept your feet planted on the ground and didn't move. You were able to stay in place because of friction. Friction is a **force** that acts against motion.

8

Friction allows you to remain in place on a hill, even though it slopes.

Friction is the force that keeps two objects like your feet and a steep hill stuck together.

Perhaps you decided to climb the hill and found that it got even steeper. At some point, you may have found yourself starting to slide downhill. But somehow you were able to stop sliding. Once again, friction was at work. In this case, friction acts as a force that slows down and may even stop a moving object. But does friction affect all moving objects the same way?

# Sliding Down

**You will need:**
- wide, smooth wooden board
- table
- variety of small objects that have at least one flat surface, such as an ice cube, eraser, match box, plastic and wooden blocks
- hand lens (optional)

**P**lace the wooden board on a table. Arrange the objects along one edge of the board. Slowly raise the edge of the board. Which object starts to slide down the board first?

Use a board that is wide enough to hold all the objects and long enough for them to slide down.

Keep raising the edge slowly until all the objects have slid down the board. Which object was the last to slide down the board?

If you feel the object that slid down the board first, you will find that it has a smoother surface than the object that slid down last. If you use a hand lens or microscope to look very closely, you will see that all objects have tiny bumps on their surfaces. Even something that looks as smooth as a piece of paper has tiny bumps on its surface.

This photograph was taken through a microscope and shows that a piece of paper is covered with tiny bumps.

There is usually less friction when two smooth surfaces move across each other. There is even less friction if one or both surfaces are slippery. Because the surface of an ice cube is both smooth and slippery, it should slide down the board first. Because ice is smooth and slippery, a skater can easily glide across its surface. Even if they stop moving their legs, skaters will still coast because there is little friction to stop them.

The more friction there is, the more slowly an object moves. At times, a person may want to increase friction. Mountain climbers wear gloves and rub them with a substance to increase friction so that their hands don't slip.

So friction affects how an object moves across a surface. But does friction depend on how an object moves across the surface?

# Moving Different Ways

**You will need:**
- sandpaper
- smooth wooden board
- cup hook
- rubber band
- ruler
- smooth, flat surface

**R**ub one edge of the board with sandpaper until it is as smooth as its surface. Screw the cup hook into the middle of an adjoining edge. Place the rubber band around the hook. Stand the board on the edge you sanded. Ask someone to pull the rubber band until the board starts moving across the floor. Measure the length of the rubber band while it is stretched and moving the board.

Now place the board so that it is flat against the smooth, flat surface. Again have someone pull the rubber band so that the board begins to move. Measure the length of the rubber band as it pulls the board across the flat surface. You should find that the rubber band stretches about the same length, whether the board is flat or on its edge.

More of the board touches the surface when it is flat than when it is on its edge, so there is more contact area. This experiment shows that friction does not depend on the size of the contact area. There is the same amount of friction no matter how the board moves along the surface. But what happens if you add some weight to the board?

# Adding Weight

**You will need:**
- board, cup hook, rubber band, flat surface, and ruler from Experiment 2
- large book

Place the board flat on a smooth surface. Ask someone to pull the rubber band until the board starts moving across the surface. Measure the length of the rubber band when it is stretched and begins to move the board.

Now place the book on the board. Again have someone pull the rubber band so that the board begins to move across the surface.

16

Measure the length of the rubber band when the board and book begin to move. Did the rubber band stretch more this time?

The rubber band should stretch more as it begins to pull both the board and the book. This means that you have to pull harder to start the board and book moving. You have to pull harder because there is more friction to overcome. Placing the book on the board adds weight. Adding weight increases the amount of friction. The more friction, the harder it is to start an object moving.

Because the box full of books is heavier, friction makes it harder to start moving it.

# What Else Can Friction Do?

Friction can keep two objects stuck together so that neither one moves. Friction can also slow down and even stop a moving object. But in a way, friction also keeps things moving. For example, when you walk, there is friction between the soles of your shoes and the ground. This friction keeps you from slipping and falling. Without this friction, you would not be able to walk as easily or get very far.

If you decide to run in your dressy shoes, you may slip and fall. If you want to run fast, you should wear sneakers. The bottoms of the sneakers give you more friction so that you do not slip and fall.

Is there anything else that friction can do besides affect how things move?

# Experiment 4

# Wearing Away

**You will need:**
- water-based paint
- brush
- three small pieces of wood
- crayon
- three different grades of sandpaper (fine, medium, and coarse)

**A**sk an adult to paint one surface on each piece of wood. Be sure that each piece gets the same amount of paint. Allow the paint to dry thoroughly. Then use the fine sandpaper to rub against one piece of wood back and forth fifty times. Did you wear away any of the paint by rubbing it with the fine sandpaper?

Rub the medium sandpaper against another piece of wood back and forth fifty times. Be sure to apply the same amount of pressure as you did when using the fine sandpaper. How much of the paint is gone this time? Do the same with the coarse sandpaper and the third piece of wood. How much of the paint does this sandpaper remove?

You can tell by feeling the three types of sandpaper that the coarse one has the roughest surface. Rubbing the wood with the coarse sandpaper produces the most friction. Friction causes things to wear away. The more friction, the more things wear away. Rubbing the wood with the coarse sandpaper produces the most friction and wears away the most paint. What else can friction do?

Friction can wear away cloth to make holes where your pants rub against things most often.

# Experiment 5

## Heating Up

**F**eel the piece of wood. Then rub the wood with the sandpaper back and forth fifty times. Immediately touch the wood where you rubbed it. Does the wood now feel warmer? Allow the wood to cool. Now rub the wood back and forth fifty times, while pressing as hard as you can. Does the wood get even warmer?

The friction from rubbing two sticks together can produce enough heat to start a fire.

The friction caused by rubbing made the wood get warmer. Friction produces heat. Pressing harder produces more friction. The more friction, the more heat is produced. This is why the wood got warmer after you pressed harder. This is also why you can warm your hands on a cold day by pressing your palms together and rubbing them quickly.

23

# Where Can You Find Friction?

So far, you have learned that friction is created when one solid object moves across another solid object. For example, you created friction when you pulled a block of wood across a flat surface and rubbed a piece of sandpaper across wood.

What happens when you move a solid object through a liquid such

as water? For example, is friction
still produced when a sailboat
moves through the water?
What happens when a solid
object moves through the air?
Is friction created when a plane
flies through the sky?

# Experiment 6

💡

# Moving in Water

Fill both bowls halfway with water. Gently place the rubber ball in the middle of one bowl and the tennis ball in the middle of other bowl. Wait until both balls stop moving. Then use your hand to start the rubber ball spinning. Time how long the ball spins.

Now do the same with the tennis ball. Which ball spins for a longer time in the water? Friction is created when objects

move

in water. Both the rubber
ball and the tennis ball slow down and then stop
spinning because of friction. But the rubber ball
has a smoother surface. The smoother surface

causes less friction. Because there is less friction, the rubber ball spins for a longer time than the tennis ball. If there is friction when an object moves across a solid or through the water, is there friction when an object moves through the air?

# Experiment 7

## Falling to the Ground

**You will need:**
- two identical pieces of paper
- transparent tape
- chair

Take one piece of paper and fold it in half from top to bottom. Then fold it in half again. The second fold should be from left to right.

Keep folding the paper, first from top to bottom and then from left to right. Stop when you cannot make another fold.

Tape the paper so that it does not unfold. Loosely crumple the second piece of paper. Stand on the chair. Hold the folded paper in one hand and the crumpled paper in the other hand. Drop them at the same time. Which one hits the floor first?

Both pieces of paper weigh the same. So why does the folded paper fall faster than the crumpled paper? When you drop them, both papers fall through the air. The air moves across both papers, causing friction. This type of friction is called **air resistance**. Air resistance slows down both papers as they fall. However, when you fold the paper, there is less of it exposed to the air.

This means that there is less air resistance to slow the paper that you folded. The folded paper falls through the air faster than the crumpled paper. Changing the shape of an object, then, can reduce air resistance.

# How Else Can You Reduce Friction?

Air resistance is a big concern of designers of cars, planes, and boats. These designers try to reduce friction so that a car will travel across the road, a plane will fly through the air, and a boat will move through the water as easily as possible.

This bike (left) is designed to reduce air resistance. This bicyclist (right) wears an aerodynamic helmet and crouches low to the bicycle to reduce air resistance.

Besides changing an object's shape, how else can you reduce friction?

# Spinning Around

**You will need:**
- modeling clay
- pencil
- tape
- empty coffee can with lid
- marbles

**A**dd a small ball of clay to each end of the pencil. Use tape to attach the pencil to the top of the lid. Place the lid over the bottom of the can. Try to spin the lid by giving the pencil a whirl. How well does it spin? Remove the lid and pencil.

Cover the bottom of the can with marbles. Place the lid on top of the marbles.

34

Try to spin the lid again. Notice that the lid spins much more easily on top of the marbles. The smooth, round surfaces of the marbles reduce friction. Because friction is reduced, it is easier for the lid to spin around the can. Many devices with moving parts have smooth, round balls to reduce friction.

A bicycle wheel has ball bearings. Like marbles, these are round and smooth and reduce friction.

# Experiment 9

# Oiling the Surface

**You will need:**
- smooth wooden board
- baby oil
- two identical plastic or wooden blocks

**S**et the wooden board on a table. Rub a light coat of oil on one half of the board. Place the two blocks along one edge of the board. Slowly raise the edge of the board. Which block starts to slide down the board first? The oil makes the board slippery. The slippery surface helps to reduce friction so that the block can move faster.

Each of these
people is using
something to
reduce friction.

Oil, grease, and wax are commonly used to reduce friction. Oil is added to engines so that their moving parts slide past each other more easily. Grease is applied to machines so that the moving parts are not slowed down as much by friction. Wax is rubbed along the bottom of skis so that they move down the slope more quickly.

Friction is a force that slows down and may even stop a moving object. Sometimes you would like to reduce friction so that you could travel down a slide or move through the water faster. At other times you would like to increase friction so that you could walk on an icy road or run to catch a ball without slipping.

# Fun With Friction

Now that you have learned what friction is, here's a fun experiment to do. You can make a piece of cardboard move across a table just as it would if there were no friction. The cardboard will seem to be floating on air.

# Floating on Air

**You will need:**
- ruler
- pencil
- cardboard
- sharp knife
- small nail
- glue
- wooden spool
- balloon
- twist tie
- smooth flat surface

**U**se the ruler to draw a square on the cardboard that is 5 inches (12.5cm) on each side. Ask an adult to use a sharp knife to cut out the cardboard square. Push a small nail through the center of the smooth side of the cardboard. Remove the nail.

Glue the wooden spool to the top of the cardboard. Make sure that the hole in the spool is over the hole in the cardboard. You should be able to see through the holes in the spool and cardboard. Allow the glue to dry thoroughly.

Blow up the balloon. Secure the twist tie around the neck of the balloon so that the air does not escape. Place the neck of the balloon over the spool.

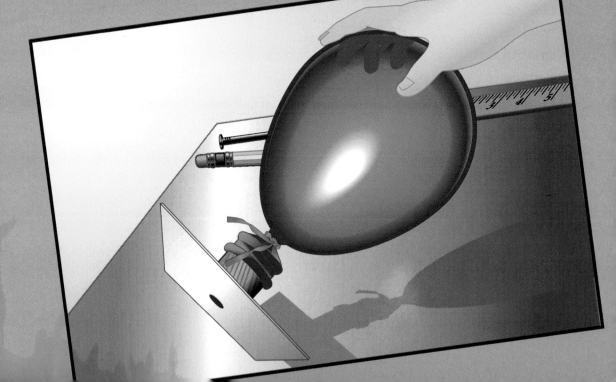

Set everything on a flat, smooth surface such as a kitchen counter top. Remove the twist tie. Give the cardboard a gentle push. The "car" should start gliding along the counter top.

Air from the balloon passes through the holes and forms a cushion of air underneath the cardboard. This cushion of air reduces the friction between the cardboard and the surface of the table. Because there is less friction, the cardboard moves more easily across the counter top. This is how a hovercraft speeds across the water.

A hovercraft rides on a cushion of air just above the water. This reduces friction so that it can move faster.

# To Find Out More

If you would like to learn more about friction, check out these additional resources.

 **Books**

Cole, Joanna. **The Magic School Bus Plays Ball: A Book About Forces.** Scholastic, 1998.

Dalton, Cindy Devine. **Force & Motion.** The Rourke Book Company, 2001.

DiSpezio, Michael Anthony. **Awesome Experiments in Force and Motion.** Sterling Publishing Company, 2000.

Willis, Shirley. **Tell Me How Fast It Goes.** Franklin Watts, 1999.

**Fear of Physics**
*http://www.fearofphysics. com/Friction/friction.html*

Try to stop a moving vehicle, such as a big red truck or a motorcycle, as it moves on a dry or icy road. Apply the brakes and see if friction will stop the vehicle before there's an accident.

**The Franklin Institute Science Museum**
222 North 20th Street
Philadelphia, PA 19103
215-448-1200
*http://sln.fi.edu*

Type in "static electricity" in the Search box. You will be led to a large number of sites. Some of them show you how to use friction to make static electricity.

**Science Museum of Minnesota**
*http://www.smm.org/sln/tf/ f/friction/friction.html*

See how an artist uses ball bearings to reduce friction and create sculptures that move smoothly.

**National Aeronautics and Space Administration (NASA)**
*http://kids.msfc.nasa.gov/ SolarSystem/Meteors/ Meteors.asp*

Learn how friction causes meteors to burn up in Earth's atmosphere.

# Important Words

*air resistance*  friction caused when an object moves through the air

*force*  a push or pull that can either start an object moving or stop it from moving

*friction*  a force that slows down and can even stop a moving object

# Index

# Meet the Author

Salvatore Tocci is a science writer who lives in East Hampton, New York, with his wife Patti. He was a high school biology and chemistry teacher for almost thirty years. As a teacher, he always encouraged his students to perform experiments to learn about science. Aware of what friction can do, he tries to keep the hull of his sailboat waxed and clean so that it moves through the water as fast as possible.

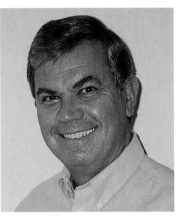